The Child's Approach to Religion

✠✠✠

The Child's Approach to Religion

By
The Rev. H. W. Fox, D.S.O., M.A.

With an Introduction by
The Right Rev. the Lord Bishop of Liverpool

SECOND EDITION

Publishers
HARPER & BROTHERS
New York and London

THE CHILD'S APPROACH TO RELIGION

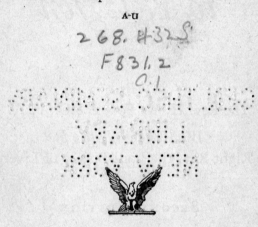

To "Margaret"
Bill *and* Ian

Contents

✠✠✠

Author's Preface
to the Second Edition

✠✠✠

THIS LITTLE BOOK WAS PUBLISHED FOURTEEN YEARS ago. Ian's father and mother, for whom it was written, are now across the Atlantic from me, and Ian himself is serving in the Royal Canadian Navy. But my publishers tell me that other parents are today finding that this book helps them to teach their children about God and about the way in which, as I believe, he may become real to them, not only in their childhood, but in the more difficult years which follow. A new edition thus gives me an opportunity to add a preface.

Coming back to what I wrote is like meeting an old friend whom I had almost forgotten; but upon renewing our acquaintance, I find that I have no wish to change anything I wrote when I said goodbye to him. The passage of years has not led me to think otherwise than I thought then. I was writing, however, in days of peace, when evil was not so obviously at large and rampant as it is today. There is now a question which John or Jane may have already begun to ask when you have told them about the kindliness of Jesus and about the fact that we can only rightly think of God as a good Father, loving good and willing good. Why then, they may say, does God let people kill and starve one another? He can't possibly like them to suffer; Why doesn't he stop them? After all, this is a question which is puzzling many of us today.

I think that we can approach what is no new problem in this way. You may tell John and Jane that God lets them and all of us do exactly as we like; he has given us the power to choose, and that is what makes us quite different from an engine or a screwdriver which have no wills of their own and can only do their work when some one else handles them as he wants; they are slaves, not free; tools, not human beings. We, however, have come into the world with wills of our own; if we use them in the line of God's will for good, all is well; if we don't, there is sure to be trouble. When John got hold of a knife, which you told him he had better not touch, and cut himself, that was his own fault and he couldn't blame you for having left it lying about. We suffer because we have not known how we ought to use or to control that freedom to choose which makes us human beings and not machines.

So far perhaps so good; but a bigger difficulty remains. Why should you and I and millions of people suffer because another person or another group of persons does wrong? It is they who are to blame and ought to suffer, and not we. In trying to explain this, we have to bring in another fact. Although each of us has an independent will, God's plan for our lives is not that each of us should live on a desert island by himself. How dull Robinson Crusoe found his life, even with his parrot for company, until Man Friday appeared! We were all born to live as members of a group, of concentric circles of groups, from the family and the school to the nation and the race. We can apply very widely what Paul said of the human body: "Whether one member suffer, all the members suffer with it." This is one of the laws of nature from which we cannot get away; common suffering is part of the price we have to pay for our freedom. "It is not," said a writer in *The Times* (London) recently, "that God is helpless in our modern situation, nor that his providence has ceased to have any relevance to human life, but that for man's ultimate good, at whatever cost to himself, he must allow the laws of cause and effect to operate." It is along this path that you can perhaps lead John's and Jane's thoughts, working from what they already know in the family to what they do not now understand in the wider world. All life is shared life. You can find many examples in ordinary everyday happenings. Lead them, I suggest, gradually by their own experience of life; it is small at present, but every day widens it. Above all, start from what you have yourself discovered, for it is only from your own discoveries that you can effectively teach your children to discover God for themselves.

May I add a further word. Some time after I wrote this book, *Tales from the Old Testament* was also published in America by Harper & Brothers. In this I tried to show how the old stories might be made to live for children of today. A second series, alas, became ashes in the Fire of London.

H. W. Fox

April, 1943

Introduction

✠✠✠

I AM OFTEN ASKED BY PARENTS AND TEACHERS TO advise them how to give first lessons to little children about Christ, the Bible, and God. In days when people were satisfied with what was known as "simple Bible teaching," made simple by very haphazardous methods, and reinforced by formal questions and answers to be learnt by heart, the task seemed comparatively easy. But now conditions have changed. In the first place we know a great deal more than we did about the direction of a child's interest, the working of his mind, and the process by which he appropriates or rejects what we offer him. And secondly we have accumulated a store of experience showing how much must often be unlearnt by those who were taught in the old way if their childhood's teaching is to develop without a serious break into a full grown faith.

One of the first results of this new knowledge and experience is to make the task of early teaching seem so difficult that many parents are tempted to abandon it to whatever expert can be found. Others, who are willing to take trouble and to read books, are greatly in need of definite guidance in a practical shape. They are still perplexed as to the sequence and form in which to make first presentations of the life of Christ, of Old Testament stories, of God in the modern world. They ask, "How shall I so instruct my child about Christ as to give him personal knowledge of a Hero, Leader, Saviour, Friend of his own?" Or, "How can I show God in all good life as my child sees life, within the vision Christ used when He saw the Father in life as it appeared to him?" Or, "If he asks me about it how can I help him to think truly, reasonably, and bravely about death?" Or, "How can I tell him the truth so that he can accept it, and find nothing in what I say which in a wider experience later on he might be led to reject?"

These and other perplexities are fully faced and wisely and courageously answered in Mr. Fox's letters to his friend. I know of no book which sets forth so clearly and attractively a course of Christian teaching definite yet sympathetic. I know of many parents, including myself, who need and want exactly what it offers. And I think I can promise that it will help them to teach not only their children, but themselves.

ALBERT LIVERPOOL

Bishop's Lodge, Liverpool
May, 1929

The Child's Approach
to Religion

✤ I ✤

A Background

IT MAY APPEAR ABSURD THAT I, WHO HAVE NEVER had the responsibility of educating children of my own, should even attempt to put forward any suggestions for the religious education of other people's children. I have, however, two excuses for my presumption. I have been asked by you to write down some of the ideas which we have discussed together, and I am not so old as to have entirely forgotten the religious education which I received in my own home. Of my religious teaching in school I shall not say anything. Perhaps for the reason that I was never at a boarding school, the religious teaching which I received at school made no impression on my mind; it was concerned only with the history of the kings of Israel and Judah and later on with the text of the Greek Testament, and these subjects were taught with the same detachment from reality as the wars of the Roses or the speeches of Cicero.

In my home, on the other hand, between the middle 'seventies and the 'eighties, I was steeped in an atmosphere of religion to an extent that probably hardly exists or is even conceivable to-day. The religious exercises of the family were frequent and regular on weekdays as well as on Sundays; the observance of Sunday was impregnated with an almost Jewish strictness; yet, although it was probably based on the restrictions of the Mosaic law, I cannot recollect that it ever appeared irksome. The literal and verbal inspiration of the Bible was taken for granted and was never questioned; an attitude of mind which was made easier by the fact that no book, either religious or secular, with whose views my father did not agree was allowed to come within our reach or even to enter the doors of our house.

We lived a life protected from the evil influences of the outside world, so far as it was possible for parents to give protection. Dancing, theatres, and even whist were banned as severely as wine and tobacco. I remember that the choice of Thackeray's *Esmond* as a holiday task was made the subject of a letter of protest to my schoolmaster; selected passages from Dickens were occasionally read aloud on winter evenings, but Shakespeare was not encouraged, and certain novels—I think they were called "stories" because the name of "novel" had a sinister sound—expurgated of "swear words" by a heavy lead pencil, were permitted as holiday reading, but only after lunch. To read a novel in the morning, I used to be told, was as bad a habit as dram drinking.

It might be supposed from this that my home life as a boy was miserable and wretched. It was certainly narrow, but I cannot remember that I felt it in the least unhappy or that its restrictions weighed upon me. A large garden, a large family, a strongly encouraged interest in nature and in "making things," a family magazine—an inheritance from an earlier generation—to which all contributed in the summer and Christmas holidays, provided outlets for physical and mental activities. I do not think I was ever inclined to doubt the rightness of the method on which my life was planned. Nothing was ever doubtful in my father's mind; there were clear lines between black and white, there was no intervening space of grey; anything on which any doubt might arise was for safety's sake discouraged and classed as evil. In ascertaining what was true and what was false, what was good and what was evil, texts from the Bible were the final infallible test. They had equal authority whether they were taken from the Old Testament or the New, and any discrepancies were conveniently explained away so that the Evangelical interpretation and the Puritan tradition should not be disturbed.

In the more intimate realm of personal and positive religion, there was little insistence—rather the reverse —upon the Church and its authority or upon the social aspects of the Christian Society. Religion meant almost exclusively the personal relation between the individual and God; salvation was a personal matter than which nothing could be more important; it seemed to have much more to do with hopes of the future life than with the conditions of the present, and it could only be securely possessed on the terms explicitly laid down by St. Paul. I do not mean to say that religion had nothing to do with conduct, but right conduct was only acceptable when it followed and did not precede a faith which was much more emotional than intellectual. The best-lived life was of no profit in the eyes of God or men; it could commend one to neither and could contribute nothing to one's chance of heaven, if it was not accompanied by a conscious apprehension of the forgiveness of sins by the death of Christ. For this reason a definite experience of "conversion" was normally necessary, as well as reassuring, and there followed also from this the bounden duty of sending missionaries to the heathen and Mohammedans, so that they might have at least a chance of escaping eternal punishment. It would be right, I think, to say that the type of religion set before us had a very large emotional content, and that we were taught to love the Lord our God with our hearts rather than with our minds.

I do not want to give the idea that the Christianity which my father and mother displayed was only formal and conventional; it was very far from that, and their lives, unharassed by theological doubts, were in truth a simple appreciation and exhibition of most of the highest Christian virtues. There was a true and positive Christian life combined with an intolerance of the teaching of those with whom they did not themselves agree, an almost Puritan sternness regarding behaviour and a rigidness of orthodox, or, in other words, evangelical, standards of belief.

I was long past the age of adolescence before I found the necessity of unlearning much which I had been taught as a boy, and before I learnt to think out the fundamental facts of Christianity instead of taking for granted what undoubtedly had been the satisfying experience of others, but what had been accepted upon external authority by myself. I have sketched these outlines of my own early religious training, not because they are matters of any interest in themselves, but because they may serve as a contrasted background to the suggestions which I am venturing to make about the way in which religious teaching may to-day be given to children in their homes and to your Ian in particular.

✦ II ✦

The Approach

THERE ARE TWO WAYS IN WHICH RELIGIOUS TEACHING can be given to children: by the example of the lives of those who surround them and by the direct and explicit teaching by word of mouth. Of these two ways the first is, I think, the more important, because it is the earliest line of approach, because it will create the deepest and most lasting impression, and because it is most often given quite unconsciously. The last thing that I want to do in writing these letters is to create any idea that I am preaching to those who know less than myself, and I will therefore quote a sentence which I came across to-day in a Jewish novel by a Swiss writer. An old rabbi is lamenting that his children, now grown up, have revolted against the authority of the teaching which he imposed upon them when young. He takes the blame on his own shoulders and says that the child can only learn from what his elders themselves really are and not from what they teach him. It is, of course, a commonplace, but I put it forward because it lies at the bottom of your task, the formation of Ian's character. Long before he was able to understand a word you said to him, he was unconsciously learning what you were to him and he to you. Impressions of what love is were being created in his mind, although it will be years before he will ever be able to put any experience of love into words, and although he will never know that he was getting his first experience

5

of love from all you did for him, from the way in which you looked at him and spoke to him when he was first lying beside you in your bed. And if he was unconscious of the impression he was receiving, I am sure that you were just as unconscious of the impression you were forming on his mind. That is where the value of these impressions lies. Because they were unconsciously produced and were unstudied, spontaneous and perfectly natural expressions of yourself, they have struck deep into him. It will always be so with him and you. When you are least conscious of creating an impression, you will probably be impressing him the most. His training will begin, and perhaps also end, by attending to what you are much more than to what you say. I think that this is borne out in our own experience, at least in mine, of our contacts with other people. They have influenced us probably least of all by what they have said; even when their words may seem to have been the moving influence, I think that if we analysed our impressions we should find that the influence really came from the attitude of mind—for want of a better word—which prompted the words and of which they were only the quite unstudied expression.

So every day Ian will be learning from what you are much more than from your words, especially when his own mind is undeveloped and when he has only begun to understand the meaning of words. He will get a conception of goodness because you are good to him and to other people; of love because you and Bill unceasingly love one another as well as him; of truth because you are unfailingly truthful; of kindliness of speech, because your words and your tones of speech are never harsh; of constancy, because you always keep your promise; of consideration for others and unselfishness because he sees these things in you. You cannot talk to him yet, nor for a long time, of these abstract virtues, but when he can understand the meaning of the words, he will know that he has really understood them all the time and that you are only giving the dress of words to the living things he has already learnt. Long before you can talk to him of God in such a way that he can understand your words—if, indeed, we ourselves know or can know anything more of Him than the fringe of Himself—he will understand something of God because of you. I think you will understand me if I say that in some sense, but in a true sense, you will be an incarnation, a human representation, of God to him, an incarnation of the best and highest values of life, of all that is most beautiful and good and true in so far as any of us can express these things.

After all, just because our personalities are human, it needed that God should show Himself in Christ as a human personality if we were to acquire any adequate, but still, perhaps, imperfect, idea of what God is. Ian cannot at first understand the meaning of Christ, much less of God, but he can understand you, he cannot help understanding you, and he will gain his own first ideas of God from his impressions of you. This is why, at least so it seems to me, the persons by whom a child is first surrounded are the most important people in the whole of his life; it is from them that he will first of all receive his right or, may be, his wrong ideas of God. If the ideas he receives are wrong, he may have to spend years of his life in unlearning them, and our purpose ought to be so to teach a child that he may never have to unlearn anything. In theory, at any rate, even though it may prove impossible in practice, all acquired knowledge ought to be an addition to that already possessed and not a subtraction of what was wrong. To plan or to undertake a system of education otherwise, with the idea that each stage in life can be kept separate from those on either side of it, that what has been learnt before need have no reference to and may be deliberately corrected by what shall be learnt afterwards, is to be condemned not only because it is a waste of time, but because it is impossible to eliminate entirely from the memory, and therefore from the character, any impression, good or bad, that has been once made. You can always add to what is imperfect, you can never eradicate altogether the effect of what is wrong.

✥ III ✥

The Kindliness of Jesus

I HAVE EMPHASIZED THIS LAST POINT, THE IMPOR-
tance of avoiding the necessity of unlearning anything, because it has a very direct bearing not only upon
what I have said of Ian gaining his first ideas of God
from what he sees in you, but also upon what I am
going to suggest may be the method of your direct and
conscious teaching as distinct from your unconscious
teaching of him. It is related to the way in which you
will teach him about Christ, about the Bible, about
prayer, and about all that goes to the making of a
Christian life and character.

You will know far better than I can when Ian begins
to be interested in stories, but that will be the moment
when you can begin to teach him about Jesus. My
idea, and probably also yours, would be to begin with
the simple stories of his wonderful acts of kindness.
May I put in here as a parenthesis, don't keep what you
tell him about Jesus for Sundays only, let it be part of
your ordinary talking to him, so that he shall not begin
to think of Sunday as entirely different, i.e., different in
kind, from other days. I suppose you and I and most
people who have had any Christian teaching have been
taught to look upon Sunday as so entirely different
from the other days of the week, a day perhaps, of
negations when we had to live quite a different kind of
life, that we have been in real danger of making a difference between our conduct on Sunday and our conduct

on Saturday or Monday. In a certain way, though it may seem absurd, I am not quite sure that we ought to connect Sunday with clean clothes or best clothes or extra good food. There is a danger in this of giving a false meaning to Sunday, for isn't its difference from other days more a difference of opportunity, that is, of degree, than of kind? Our plan of ordered life makes any rearrangement of the week quite impossible, but mightn't it be good if we could reset our arrangements and, say, have our church services every five days or six days, or eight days if you prefer, so that they would be held as often on a Monday or a Wednesday as on a Sunday? At any rate, we should then have a chance of breaking the convention that a different standard of conduct is proper to Sundays from that which we allow ourselves, say, on Wednesdays or Thursdays. You see what I am driving at, that Ian should not begin to think about God or Christ having a special connection with one day of the week above the others. It is one of the things we don't want him to have to unlearn, because this particular bit of unlearning is rather difficult and may have bad consequences.

There is another parenthesis which I want to put in here. Never teach Ian anything which is not part of your own quite definite religious, conviction and experience, that is, as something which he himself must believe as true, whether you believe it or not. For one thing he will probably not be long in finding out that there is a difference between what you believe and what you tell him he ought to believe; when he discovers this there will be a conflict of ideas in his mind; he will have to begin the horrible process of unlearning, and there is a risk that he may also begin to distrust everything you tell him and that in consequence your teaching will be robbed of a great part of the effect which you are wanting to produce. You will be undermining your own authority as a teacher. At the same time, however, in the course of your teaching, you will have to bring to his notice a number of things about which neither you nor any one else can speak as matters of your own experience. He will soon be asking you thousands of questions to which you cannot give any cut and dried, definite and dogmatic answers. Don't attempt to do so. It will be, I think, far better for you to say frankly: "I don't know and no one else knows for certain," or "This is what I think about it, but then there are other people who don't think as I do," or "we will try and find out together all about it." I am not sure that it is good for him, even when he is quite small, to think that you know everything and are infallible. While, as I have said, you can in a real way represent God to him in your own lives, infallibility is one of the Divine characteristics none of us can represent. Sooner or later, again, he is bound to find out that you are not infallible, and the effect of this discovery, if he is not prepared for it, may be to produce a severe moral shock to his character. A shock of this kind is one of the very things you will want to avoid, for it may go a long way to undermining the complete confidence that you want to create and maintain for ever unshaken between yourselves and him.

After these two parentheses, let us come back to your beginning to teach Ian about Jesus. I suggest that you should begin with the quite simple stories of his kindness. For one reason they are the simplest things for him to understand, but, for another and more important reason, it was in this way that the people of his own day first of all came to know anything about him; it was the way in which the children of Palestine learnt about him from their mothers. I suggest that you should tell Ian about him just as they did. I doubt if you can improve on the original line of approach. I am sure, for instance, that the Palestine mothers didn't begin with the stories about his birth, the visits of the wise men and the shepherds; and as for the story of his death and resurrection they could not have talked of events which had not then happened. The birth stories had happened thirty years ago, probably before the mothers themselves were born, and even if they then had any widespread currency, which I doubt, they would have been altogether unreal as actual events to the small children; they would have been so far outside of and unrelated to their own experience that they would only have conveyed as much or as little truth as fairy stories. I don't want to convey the impression that these early stories must not be classed as representing historical events, but only that they would, I think, appear to a child so strange and so foreign to the things that are happening to himself that he would be led to place Jesus, so to speak, right off the human map. And that is an impression which we want at all costs to avoid.

The first impression that we want Jesus to make in Ian's mind is that he was a very real and a very kind man. Add that he had a wonderful power of healing sick people and helping people in trouble. Don't worry Ian about "miracles." I think you would be right in rationalizing what we call miracles as much as possible and in setting Jesus on an absolutely human plane. Very few, if any, people during his life-time ever thought of him as God; that idea only came later, and I think it must come later for Ian. This rationalizing of "miracles" is much easier to-day than it used to be, because there is now a considerable amount of evidence to show that certain persons still have remarkable gifts of healing, which are parallel in kind, if not in degree to those which Jesus possessed. For the moment, therefore, leave out the three stories of his raising dead persons to life; those had better come later as well as the stories of the demoniacs, of the multiplication of the bread, and of the storm on the lake. In speaking of the wonderful powers of healing, you may say that only a few persons ever had this power, but that some persons still have it: this is perfectly true, and if you can put it in this way you will, I think, make Jesus a real human being, as real and as human, say, as Bill or your chauffeur, Jones.

That is the first impression I want you to make, but along with that, and not separated from it, Jesus' extraordinary kindness of heart. He was never too busy or too tired to attend to anyone who needed his help; he never took any money for what he did, he did it always for love; he was sorry for anyone who was in trouble and did his very best to cure and help them. If a sick man was brought to him he would stop anything else that he might be doing in order to make him better and happier. I think that without your pointing a moral to each story the moral will come quite naturally. There is an extraordinarily infectious effect about goodness whether we see it or hear of it; it somehow stirs our ambitions to go and do the same thing. Be content, to begin with, to tell all these stories of kindness in all their varieties—and there are quite a large number of them—over and over again so that Ian may become thoroughly familiar with them without being tired of them, and so that in his own language he can repeat them to you quite naturally. Then I think you may expect to find that quite naturally and spontaneously—or, as the theologians might say, by the work of the Spirit of Jesus or of God, which is really quite true—Ian's mind will be filled with the wish to do, so far as he can, the same kind things, and to be unselfish in his kindness, because he is really sorry for people who are sick or in trouble, and is thinking more of them than of himself and is thinking them much more important than himself. If you are successful in teaching him this, it will be perhaps the most important thing he will ever learn.

You will now be in a position to go on to the teaching which Jesus gave by his words. This, again, is the right order, for it was, I believe, the example of his character that drew people to listen to Jesus and gave him the opportunity of speaking to them. Here you will have a much wider field to work on. But I should begin by linking the teaching by example to the teaching by words. Here is an illustration of what I mean: You have been concentrating on the kindliness of Jesus; follow up this beginning by the story which we call the story of the good Samaritan, only, of course, you won't call it that and you won't confuse Ian's mind with the particular differences between priest and levite and Samaritan. While later on their respective positions will add force to the story, it is enough to begin with to say that two men who might have been expected to help the man who had been robbed and hurt were so selfish that they took no notice of him while a complete stranger took a tremendous lot of trouble to help him. It was Jesus who was always doing kind things like that and who wanted other people to "go and do likewise" to persons who had no claim upon them and perhaps actually disliked them. Another quite easy story of the same kind is that of the shepherd and the lost sheep, either from Matt. xviii. 12, or Luke xv. 4-6. This you can largely elaborate, but I think the point of the two stories is the same, the taking of trouble to give help, at least that is enough for the present.

I think you can safely leave over for some time those parables which can have no special reference to Ian's own immediate experience, such as the sower, the two houses, and the judgment parables (e.g. the rich man and Lazarus, the tares in the field, the ten virgins, and even that of the talents). All these will fit in later on quite naturally. But you can now quite well come to the two or three stories which will teach him about forgiveness; the first part of the prodigal son and the two debtors. Here is something fresh for Ian to learn of what Jesus, whose character is beginning to become real to him and to inspire him unconsciously, would like him to think about other people. You will see I am suggesting that for the present you should still take these stories quite simply on the human side. Remember that I am acting on the idea that you have not attempted to teach him anything about God; that will come very soon, but not quite yet. Take the first of these stories, then, as a story of what forgiveness is in an extreme and therefore strong case. A rotten and ungrateful boy—run away from a good home—coming back and welcomed by his father just as though he had never behaved so badly—a forgiveness that was shown in a very practical way. But in order to safeguard yourself, you had better make it clear to Ian that forgiveness on the father's part was accompanied by a complete change in the attitude of the son towards his father. Similarly you can take the story of the two debtors, and for our present purpose point out that because you have very often forgiven Ian, it is up to him to forgive anyone who has in any way hurt him.

✦ IV ✦

The Idea of God

NOW I THINK WE MUST COME TO WHAT AND HOW
you are going to teach Ian about God. I have been
putting it off not only because it is very difficult to explain Him aright and impossible to understand Him
fully, but because our best and most complete way of
understanding Him is through Jesus Christ, and it
was, therefore, necessary to begin with Jesus. The
difficulty is great enough for an adult, let alone a child.
Any idea that we can have of God must be imperfect
and incomplete, but it does not follow that it must be
incorrect. While He enters upon the plane of human
life, yet in His fulness He is beyond it, and it is in
this "beyondness" that our difficulty lies, since our own
ideas and the language in which only we can express
those ideas are limited by our experience on the plane
of human life, and any conception or verbal expression
of the "beyondness" can only be approximate to the
whole of God's being. How little or how nearly
approximate we cannot say, but we have to recognize
that our knowledge of God can only be approximate
and that the very idea of God makes it as inevitable
that He should be beyond the grasp of our human
mind as it is that the fulness of what you and Bill are
should be beyond the grasp of Ian's infantile and as
yet undeveloped mind.

At the same time, it would be only a mockery of our
human personality if God were so entirely beyond our

grasp as to be entirely unknowable by us and unrelated
to our experience. Our possible knowledge of Him, therefore, while it is and must be imperfect, is and must be at
the same time adequate. Now, if we want to escape the
danger of unlearning whatever we may have been taught
about God, our task must be to combine the imperfect
with the adequate, to avoid the confusion of the incorrect
with the incomplete. We have to relate the shadow to
the substance, the reality to the mystery, and at the same
time we have to remember that nothing is easier or more
dangerous than to teach the shadow as though it were
actually the substance. It is, however, possible that this
difficulty may appear greater to the adult mind than it is
in fact to the child, or at least to certain children in particular. It is not quite uncommon to find in children an
apprehension, whether it is imaginary or real does not
for the moment matter, of the invisible which has been
lost by the sophisticated adult mind. Thus some children
have a definite experience of an "invisible playmate" who
is very real to them, to whom they can give a name and
whom they can describe, but whom they never see and
of whom they are very shy of talking. In this way it is
possible that the idea of an invisible God and His constant presence with us may not be so strange to them as
we may suppose.

In approaching this subject, let me come back for a
moment to what I have already said about the need that
whatever we impart to others must come out of our own
experience. Before you can tell Ian anything at all useful
about God, you must have a personal idea of your own
of what God is, an idea that is at any rate approximate
to truth, although it cannot contain the whole truth
about Him. Each one of us, I suppose, has his own way

of approaching the idea or the conception of God, and we can only exchange our experiences on the chance that the experience of one person may supplement that of another. That is all that I can do or dare attempt to do here, to pass on to you some of my own ideas of God, mostly very crude and very obvious, as He appears to me. They are the result of a good deal of unlearning as well as learning and, when once one begins to unlearn, there is always a risk that one may throw overboard too much, something that is of real value with that which is of none or little worth.

We being what we are, human personalities, must, I believe, inevitably think of God in terms of personality. I do not see otherwise how we are to conceive of Him in any adequate way whatever. He must have in Himself whatever corresponds to our Ego or our self. His Ego may, and does, interpenetrate and influence mine and yours, but is distinct from mine and yours, as yours and mine are distinct from one another, although in a lesser degree they too may interpenetrate and influence each other. Every time I meet you, or anybody else, something of you influences me; I am not the same as if I had not met you. You remain yourself although something of you has come from you to me and has influenced me in one way or another, and I, on the other hand, remain myself. That something of you which has influenced me is nothing in itself physical; it has probably come across to my Ego by physical or semi-physical means, your hand, your mouth, or your word, your eyes or your look; but it is you and not they which have influenced me. The line of thought that I am trying to follow here is that of distinct personalities which exist apart from any body of flesh and bones of three dimensions. This three-dimensional body is only a very temporary shell or vehicle or dwelling-house for our Ego, which, we may take it here for granted, exists independently of the body, and will continue to exist when this body is dust or whatever else it may become. Now this idea gives me my first approximate idea of God, a distinct personality existing apart from any physical form or frame, an independent Ego who, while He is distinct, can impart Himself to you and me and everybody else. The degree in which I can resist or yield to this imparting of Himself, although a vital factor in the development of my Ego, is another matter which we need not discuss here, or at any rate at present.

Now, just because we have got into the habit of thinking of our own and other people's personalities as inseparably connected with our physical bodies, with the colour of our hair and eyes, the shape of our nose and mouth, with the way we walk, the way we speak, we find it very difficult not to connect our idea of God with the image of a physical person. The very term "Father" may become misleading because we fail to realize that the term, too, is only an approximate description of one aspect of His character. Here for a moment we can come straight back to Ian. Never attempt to show him a picture of God; I myself have seen pictures purporting to represent Him, an aged, bearded man, head, hands, arms and legs complete. Nothing could be a greater travesty of God, nothing could be more dangerous to the religious development of a child than for him to look at a picture of this kind. But I am sure you are never likely to make this mistake. I cannot help thinking that there was more in the second Commandment than the prohibition of idolatry. The making of images to represent God was forbidden because no image made by man could ever remotely resemble God; in the attempt to represent Him in a three-dimensional shape, men would convey not only an incomplete but an absolutely erroneous idea of God.

My second approximate idea of God is that in His personality He must be better than the best which anyone, or at any rate which I myself, can conceive. If this were not so, then I and not He should be God. If my own standard of truth or beauty or goodness were the highest, not only should I need no God, but I should not even imagine Him. In His character there must be a "beyondness," something more than is in my own character, or than what I can conceive my character ought to be at its highest and best. Again, come back, as an illustration of what I mean, to yourselves and Ian. At the present moment you are living on a much wider mental and moral plane than is even possible for him to conceive in the very limited experience of his mind. Your ideas of beauty are far more highly developed than his; the opportunities which you seize for expressing your kindliness of heart are far more numerous and greater than any that are as yet open to him; your knowledge of things, your embrace of truth is greater than his, and it could not be otherwise. At the same time this imperfection of appreciation of beauty or goodness or truth is not for one moment a fault for which you blame him; it is in the very nature of his being at present. It is quite enough for you that he should prefer pretty things to ugly things; you will give him opportunities of seeing beautiful things, and by setting beautiful things before him and surrounding him with beautiful things you will train him up to an increasingly higher standard of beauty. It is enough for you that he should want to learn and respond to you as you teach him to read and write and do his sums; it would be absurd for you to expect him to know to-day one thousandth part of what you know. It is enough that he should be kind and gentle and affectionate, obedient and truthful, brave and persevering in a constantly increasing degree, so that when he is your age he may be as you are.

But—and this is my point—there is in you a "beyondness" in comparison with himself; he cannot understand it, he doesn't worry about it, he is content that you should in every way be beyond him. Indeed, if this were not so, if it were possible to imagine that his mental and moral standards were equal to your own, or yours to his, not only would you be utterly unable to help him, to inspire him, or to lead him up to higher standards, but he would already have no respect for you, and your relation and Bill's to him as father and mother would be only physical, and would have no moral content whatever. All this, however, is little more than by way of illustrating my suggestion that, if a God exists for us at all, He must possess moral characteristics which are beyond and superior to our own.

The third attribute which I give to my idea of God, to this Personality in whom are the supreme and absolute moral values, is that He is entirely independent of any of our ordinary human ideas of space or time. It is perhaps impossible for us to familiarize ourselves with this idea, since it is entirely foreign to any experience of which we are conscious, for we are human beings who ourselves occupy a three-dimensional space, and who are accustomed to measure our experiences by minutes, days, and years, who cannot conceive of a fourth dimension, and to whom any period of time which it takes the light of even the nearest star to reach our eyes is so great as to be meaningless.

Nevertheless, somehow or another, as best we may and so far as is possible, it is, I think, essential to put out of our minds all ideas of time and space when we try to think of God. It is very hazardous even to attempt any illustration of a fact which is entirely outside our physical experience and to which no parallel within that experience can be given; there is all the danger of an illustration suggesting a wrong set of ideas. However, I will take the risk and suggest two examples, probably quite unscientific because I know no science, of the way in which we may be apparently independent of time and space. I always have a curious feeling when I am in Geneva or elsewhere within half a dozen kilometers of the French frontier. In Switzerland the clocks are set according to Central European time, in France by Greenwich time. I take the tram from Geneva to a village over the border and I arrive by the clock at an hour before I have left my starting point. You can get the same impression of the nonexistence of time when you are listening in the evening in London to a broadcast from Australia describing the dawn of the next day.

In a rather different way I can imagine that from an airship you would get the idea of your independence of space. You would feel—and the higher you were above the earth the stronger the feeling would be—that you were somehow separate from the earth, which was whirling on independently of your own existence. Or, in a railway train it is quite easy to get the impression, as you look out of the carriage window, that it is the countryside that is moving, while you are the observer in a fixed position. Of course these illustrations are really quite inadequate, and we shall have to fall back on the best mental conception we can get of the fact that God Himself is limited neither by time, past, or future; that while He is present with us in space at any particular point, He is not more with us or less with us than He is with friends in the far West of Canada or on the plains of India, at the same moment in time as we reckon time. This is to say that we must get rid of the idea that God is more present on the altar of a church than He is in the church porch, or more present in a church than He is in your home or in your office, on the street or in the countryside. If we hold any idea of this kind, it is an idea that we should get rid of as quickly as possible, for it vitiates the very nature of God, and to vitiate His nature, to conceive of Him in a false idea, cannot but have a dangerous effect on our relation towards Him and thus upon our own personal character.

I do not, of course, pretend for one moment that all I have said about the conception of God is anything more than the merest outline; but although even as an outline it is incomplete, I do not think that it contains anything that is incorrect or misleading, and I think it may serve as a foundation upon which you can base your teaching Ian about God. But how shall you begin so apparently difficult and bewildering a subject? Once more I suggest that you shall work from the known to the unknown. Ian already knows something about Jesus Christ, and there will be your starting point. It is the direction in which St. Paul led the thought of his friends when he used to tell them, "God was in Christ," and these four words contain the whole sum of Christian theology. Ian is familiar with the wonderfully kind things that Jesus used to do, and I suggest that you should now emphasize the point of which you will have already spoken, that Jesus did not take any credit to himself for the powers he possessed of doing good and kind things; he did not wish to attract attention to himself by any of his works of healing, indeed he was in the habit at times of withdrawing himself from the crowds lest they should take too much notice of him. The power was in him, it is true, but it came to him from outside—"God was in Christ." He referred this power to an outside Agency, of whom he most often spoke as his "Father." (But do not begin by using to Ian the word "Father" as applied to God, since it may cause a confusion of ideas in his mind.)

I wonder whether in beginning to talk to Ian along this line it would be at all helpful to use one or two illustrations. How would it be to show him one day a railway engine, pointing out how beautifully it is made, its boiler, its wheel and rods, and all the rest of it? Then, why do the wheels go round so that it can drag the train? Because there is something in the engine, which is not part of the engine, that gives it power; without steam the engine can do nothing. Or perhaps you might take as an illustration your radio for it only conveys the voice of the speaker in the studio and it is not the voice itself; unless the electric current is there, the radio set is nothing more than a few pieces of wood and glass and metal. The real power which makes the voice heard is unseen.

Here may I throw out a further suggestion in passing: create and keep in Ian's mind the sense of wonder. Let him know that there are things which neither you nor he can understand; you see the effects of the things, but not the things themselves. "The wind bloweth, but thou canst not tell whence it cometh or whither it goeth." I suppose that even Captain Peter Eckersley can't explain the whole of the method of the radio waves, and that even he wonders at it. Teach Ian to wonder, for I think this sense of wonder will help him to grasp what I have called the idea of "beyondness" and to realize that there are lots of "beyond" things, and I hope that there will always be both for him and for us.

But to come back, a simpler illustration may help. You suggest that Ian should do something. He obeys and it is he that does it, but he does it on the impulse of your suggestion, because of something outside himself. If it is to do some kind action, he really has no right to take any credit to himself for what he does; he might, of course, have resisted, and his non-resistance to your suggestion is all that he can in any way be proud of. The real credit for the kind action is due to a power outside himself. The illustration supposes a great deal of idealism; Ian is only a human boy and you and I are human, too, and it is very difficult even for us never to take credit to ourselves for our virtues when perhaps our only virtue is that we have not resisted a suggestion or an impulse outside ourselves; and that, after all, is a very small thing to be proud of. But whether you use these illustrations or any others that may occur to you or none at all, the idea that we want to impress is that there was a force, an agency, an impulse, a something, a Someone that was not Jesus, yet was in Jesus, that enabled him to heal and help other people and to be kind to them. If he can grasp the fact, tell Ian you can't explain it; it is just a fact, which I think he must now take because you tell him it is a fact, in the same way as he must believe you when you tell him about the steam in the engine or the electric force in the radio. There are certain facts which he must at present take upon your authority, and this is all right, so long as they are really facts and are not false statements which later on he will have to unlearn. This "beyondness," this "otherness" of God is a fact which his experience as he learns more will only confirm. If you have been able to establish this, you can go on to point out to Ian that this outside "impulse" always led Jesus to do kind and never unkind things, to help people and never to hurt them; therefore, the "impulse" itself was good. Then the next step can come at once; this "impulse" was always in Jesus everywhere; not only sometimes or in one special place. It was in him every day, morning and afternoon, indoors and out of doors, as Ian will have learnt as you have told him the stories with all the details your imagination— which, by the way, is not untruthful—has suggested. More than this, other people did the same kind things, and they did them by the same "impulse" at the same time as Jesus, but in different places at the same time. That is part of the wonderfulness of this "impulse," that it can be active everywhere at once.

Now, I think, if Ian has any of these ideas, however faintly, in his mind, you may give a name to this "impulse." You may say that it is what we call "God." On the other hand you may have thought it better to begin by using the word "God" earlier, and to have linked the ideas to the word or name. On the whole I should myself prefer to begin with the ideas, and then when the ideas are grasped to fix them to the name; you will have dis-

covered the phenomena, you will have established the
reality, and then you will be quite safe in crystallising
them in a name.

If I have at all suceeded in making my meaning clear,
I think you yourself will now see the method which I
have been following. I have tried to establish three approximate but fundamental ideas which are to be found
in the being of God. I have linked them to Jesus Christ's
own experience of God, and it is, then, from that experience that I have suggested you may have been able to
bring some idea of God by degrees within the compass
of Ian's mind.

V

God as Father

THE NEXT STEP FORWARD WILL LEAD US AGAIN FROM Jesus Christ's own experience of God to that experience of Him which may be Ian's and our own. It is the experience which is to be found in the use of the name "Father"; this name upon the lips of Jesus is much more common than that of "God." He used it most commonly to express not only his own experience, but the experience which he wanted his friends to have. At the same time I think we need to understand carefully the meaning with which Jesus used this name; we need to avoid attaching to it any of the meaning which we express when we use it of merely physical generation. In the use Jesus made of the word there was nothing of that, and our difficulty lies in the fact that we often use the word quite indiscriminately to describe a physical relation and a quality of character. This latter is the only use of the word which we can apply to God.

So far as I can understand it, this was the meaning of the word in the mind of Jesus. He was conscious of God, this personality outside himself, this fulness of love and wisdom and power. He cast about and found, perhaps unconsciously—or it may have come to him in a flash of imagination—that the most perfect human relation within his own experience was that of a father to his child. He might have used the word "lover" like some of the mystics; he might have used the word brother or mother, but he didn't, he chose the word "Father." The home of the carpenter at Nazareth must have been built up in conditions of wonderful happiness, for it left memories of wonderful happiness. Need we go any further to discover the source of this experience? Jesus thought of all the careful foresight and provision, of the suggestions and directions for the day's work, of the inspiration of the presence which it needed no spoken word to express, of the correction and the discipline which were never harsh and which might be conveyed by the mere glance of the eye or the movement of a hand, of the complete confidence which existed between the father and the sons, of the assumption of responsibility which the father undertook for any actions performed in obedience to his directions, of the absolute fairness of his judgments and criticism, of the reverence which he commanded by what he was, of the strong love which was embodied in him.

Am I wrong in thinking that it was because of all this that Jesus chose the name "Father" to give to God? It was the expression of the most ideal human relation that he knew. The name "God" always seems to me a little aloof and cold; "Father," on the other hand, may express the very heights and depths of affection on either side. Yet to our ultra-modern ears even "Father" may seem a little formal, stiff, and cold, and may fail to express the real content of what was in the mind of Jesus when he chose it and as he used it. Just because you know me and will not think I am wantonly irreverent, I am daring to say that I think our word "Daddy" comes nearest to what Jesus had in mind, and that he used it as a sort of pet name for

God. There is something to me in the use of that word, when I hear a boy or girl use it to their father, that tells me that there is a relation between the two which is as nearly perfect as possible, and that all is well. Use may stale it into cant, but I think it runs less risk of becoming the slave of a convention than most other words that we could use.

I like to think that it was some such idea as this that it conveyed to the mind of Jesus. You might take some of the chapters of the Gospels and make the experiment whether his use of the world does not fit in with the way in which I have dared to interpret it. But in any event I want you to avoid putting into Ian's mind an idea that the attitude of Jesus towards God had anything material or physical in it at all. Again we come back to a point which I suggested some way back, that any idea which our human minds may conceive about God can only be approximate, to which I add here that any words which we can use to express that approximate idea can in the same way only be approximate. We have, therefore, to use only one part of the meaning that is ordinarily conveyed by the word "Father." In applying it to God we must discard all the physical part of that meaning, keeping only its moral content and remembering that, as Jesus used it, he wished to describe the fact that the relationship which he conceived himself to hold towards all that he knew as God could be most nearly and most appropriately expressed by the word "Father," interpreted by the moral relationship ideally existing between a human son and a human father. This at least is the meaning of the term as it seems to me.

Although it may appear difficult to make this interpretation clear to Ian, I suggest that it is this idea that you should have in your mind as you begin to teach him that Jesus called God "Father," associating the word with all that his own father is morally to Ian, and as you go on to tell him that Jesus wanted his friends also to call God their Father and to think of Him above all else as their Father.

✠ VI ✠

Prayer

IT IS BY A VERY NATURAL SEQUENCE THAT WE COME from the thought of God as Father to the subject of prayer. If I have been at all right in suggesting that the meaning of the word even in a remote and imperfect way corresponds to "Daddy," one pictures almost at once communication between two personalities—I use deliberately a rather vague and neutral phrase. The line of approach I think that I should take here is to tell Ian of Jesus's talking with God and thinking about Him towards whom he felt as a boy towards his father. These are some of the points—Jesus going away alone; sometimes away into the country, on a hillside, in the fields; sometimes in a small room in a house where he might be quiet and alone (does not his suggestion in Matt. vi. 6 reflect a piece of his own practice?); sometimes after dark when everyone else had gone to bed, because until then he had not been able to be a minute alone; or at other times he could remember his Father in the middle of a crowd in a street (see Mark vii. 34), or when he used to go to church.

But he did not think of praying only in a special place or at a special time or on a special day; he remembered that God his Father was always with him; although he never saw Him with his eyes, as he saw all his friends, that made not the least difference. What did Jesus do when he got away alone like this? For one thing he just thought of God and kept on thinking about Him, exactly as Ian often simply thinks about either of you, how wonderfully good and kind He could not help being. Very likely Jesus seldom spoke a single word aloud as he prayed, but his mind was full of thoughts about God his Father. Then he would want to think of people and things in the same good way as God his Father thought about them. He would go over in his mind all that had happened to him during the day, the things and people he had found difficult, the things and people that had made him happy, and he would remind himself that he wanted to do what God wanted—"to do God's will"—and nothing else, for that was certain to be right. But what did God want him to do? He would think all that out. And sometimes he was so happy that he couldn't help saying to God, perhaps out loud, how happy he was.

At other times he would think of his friends, what would be the best things they could have; and the best of all that he could think of for them and for himself would be that they might know more of how good God was. Sometimes while he was thinking like this he might be standing up or walking about, sometimes he might kneel down or sometimes sit down wherever he might be, especially if he were very tired, for if your body is tired or aching it is not very easy to think and keep on thinking while you are in an uncomfortable position. It did not really matter what his position was, if only he could keep on thinking of God. Sometimes his eyes would be wide open (see again Mark vii. 34) or sometimes shut; that, too, didn't really matter, only we find it is easier to think of God and to talk to Him when we can shut out of our sight the things in a room or out of doors which might make us think of them and not of God. Sometimes, if we had been near him, we should not have heard him speak a single word; he would be thinking silently. At other times he would find it helped him more to put his thoughts into words which he said out loud; speaking out loud might make his thinking more clear and definite. But nothing of all this mattered in the least to God; he didn't need to use a single word to make his thoughts known to God; God could read his mind, just as sometimes Ian will know what you are thinking without your saying a word.

If you will go over in your mind what I have written in these two paragraphs, I think you will find that I have included most of the parts into which we divide our prayers—meditation or recollectedness of God, thanksgiving, personal petitions and intercessions for others. Of course I have not used these expressions which we are apt by custom to connect with formal acts; on the contrary I have tried to give them plain and simple meanings. I think it is along such a line of thought as this that you will most wisely and successfully begin to teach Ian about prayer. At the same time I have tried to emphasize the necessity that you should not connect Ian's prayers with any particular time of day or day of the week, or with any particular place or attitude of body. I want him to realize from the very first that, like Jesus, he can keep in mental touch, can communicate with God as Father, can pray to Him anywhere and at any time. This is a fact which we ourselves have perhaps learnt in later life, but there is no reason why Ian should not learn this at the very beginning of his life; indeed, there is every reason why he should.

Another thing I have tried to emphasize is that Ian,

again from the very first, should avoid beginning the habit of thinking of prayer only as asking God for things he wants. This conception of prayer is very mean and mentally impoverishing if you stop to think of it and to consider the parallel of Ian's talks with either of yourselves. What a hopeless idea he would have of you if in his mind you and Bill were always and only the "givers" and he always the "asker." So much has this aspect of prayer been exaggerated, and so much disappointment has come from misunderstanding this aspect, that I am inclined to lay very little stress upon it at the first, until Ian has got the really big idea of God firmly in his mind, the idea that God can be to him all and exactly that which He was to Jesus. If we take this wide and, as I believe, really true view of prayer, it will open out a wonderfully satisfying view of God Himself and of what He and we may be to each other.

There remains the question of any form or words of prayer which you should teach Ian. We have to avoid the danger—a deadly one—of forms becoming formal. Therefore I think there should be as great a variety of forms as possible, so that every time he uses them they shall come to him with freshness. I am not at all sure that it would not be a good plan for you and Ian to draw up some of your own forms of prayer together. "What shall we talk about to God our good Father to-day?" Then use quite informally and in ordinary language what you and he have suggested to one another.

Or there is another plan which you might try. Why should not Ian's evening prayers be sometimes a talk between you and him, reminding him that although he can only see you, his unseen Father is also there, listening to all that you are talking about together, "What a wonderful Father He is!" With God as the unseen listener, go over what Ian has done during the day; the moments when he has had some special enjoyment; let him say: "thank you, Father," for this happiness; and the moments when things haven't gone quite well and he has been naughty, "I'm so sorry I did or said this, that, or the other"; then, "God knows that I am sorry, just as you do, and He forgives me just as you have forgiven me, or just as the father in the story of the boy who ran away from home and came back again to find his father waiting for him and loving him as much as ever." But he will want to avoid doing what by now he will know God his Father does not want him to do; that is hard, so together you and he will remind yourselves that God is not only outside of him but within him as He was in Jesus, and will help him to do the right things that he finds so hard to do. And before you stop, you will talk of his friends, the people he has met during the day or about whom you have told him, the maids and everyone he has to do with. "What shall we wish for them? what would be the really best things they can have," putting some things aside and suggesting others? Then perhaps a little later on he may ask you: "When am I going to say my prayers?" "You have already said them." "When? How?" And will he not have covered the whole field of prayer, without the least unreality or formalism?

One further word, as Ian learns about prayer, let him not only be quite simple, but very definite in what he says or thinks. So do not let him get into the habit of using that very vague and rather lazy word "bless." It is too vague to mean very much, and I am afraid we often use it to save ourselves the trouble of thinking out what are the really best things we wish for our friends, and what exactly we should like God to do for them. We want Ian to be very definite and clear in his prayers, because by taking a little trouble they may become a great reality to him.

✠ VII ✠

The Cross

LET US NOW COME BACK TO THE STORY OF JESUS, and I think we may begin to talk to Ian about the death of Jesus and of some part at any rate of its meaning. We will try and do it quite simply and naturally without the least tinge of dogma or theology either in our own minds or in his. We will take it in the sequence of the story and as a plain historical fact as it appeared to the people who first of all witnessed it or heard of it.

I would suggest your taking as your own starting point what Jesus said as it is reported in Mark viii. 34 and 35, and what I think we may be quite certain lay behind it, although it is not reported, in the experience of himself and of those persons to whom he spoke. They had seen from time to time a little procession, soldiers and police surrounding a man who was being led off to punishment for robbery or some other crime. Those were very cruel times, and the man was to be punished by being put to death, by being fastened to two cross pieces of wood, usually, I think, by cords, and by being left hanging there until he died of starvation. The man who was in the centre of the procession was forced to carry the two planks of wood on which he was to die. This must have been a fairly familiar scene in those days, especially in or near Jerusalem, and it is of this that Jesus speaks.

There are bad people in the world as well as good, and as Ian gets older he will find that there are always people who will want him to do unkind things. (I say "unkind" because it is more concrete than a general term like "wrong," and in teaching Ian we must be very definite and use words which will convey as concrete ideas as possible.) They will make it difficult for him to be always doing kind things; in a way they may try to punish him for it, and make him suffer; and before he is much older he will find out that kind people suffer for being kind as well as bad people for being bad. Ian must be prepared to suffer for being kind, just as much as he would naturally suffer if he were punished for having done something wrong. Only, this kind of suffering is much harder to bear because it is so unfair, and the sense of its unfairness adds to the suffering. Ian, however, will be determined to do the kind things which God his good Father wants him to do, and he must be ready, like the man in the story you have just told him, to suffer. But there is for Ian this great difference; instead of, like that man, being forced to carry his cross and be crucified as a punishment for having done something wrong, Ian, as it were, will have to take up his cross of his own accord and to suffer of his own choice, because he chooses to be kind rather than unkind, no matter what unpleasant things other people may say of him or think of him. I suggest that it is in some such way as this you may begin to bring into Ian's mind the idea of what the cross means.

Then on another day you may come straight to the story of Jesus and his cross, after you have thus prepared the ground. Here is the story of another procession; it is Jesus this time who is in its centre, who is carrying the wood for his cross, and who is going to suffer and to be put to death, not, however, because he has done anything bad, but because bad men hated him, and because he tried to stop them doing the bad things which they liked to do. He could quite easily have avoided all the suffering by agreeing to do the things that other people did; he could have chosen the bad instead of the good, but that would not have been what God his Father, who always chose good and who was inspiring him with good, would have wished. Therefore, Jesus deliberately put aside the easy way of life and chose to suffer and to give up his life, to "take up his cross," in order to show how tremendously important is the good way of life. In his opinion it was better to choose the good way of life, even at the cost of dying, rather than continue to live in a bad way of life. It was this that he wanted to show everybody else; he wished to inspire them by his example to make the same choice of a good life, although for us to-day it very rarely means dying for the sake of our choice, or even suffering to anything like the same extent as Jesus.

For the moment I think that this is the aspect of the death of Jesus upon which I should especially insist. I doubt if it is wise to play too much upon Ian's emotions by telling all the details of the crucifixion, and I think I should avoid showing him any pictures of the passion and death of Jesus. It is enough to make the fact of the death and this first reason for it quite clear. We do not want to bring forward the sentimental or emotional aspects of it, so as to excite Ian's emotions at the expense of his grasping the reality of the fact and thus its primary meaning, as at least that meaning appears to me, that the choice of the good was for Jesus the most important thing in the world, and that he wished to make this so clear to all the world that he deliberately chose to die rather than to continue to live by choosing a low and bad standard of life.

For the moment I want you, therefore, to create the one impression on Ian's mind that the Jesus who is inspiring him to do kind things is an example to him of the importance of a kind and good life, that it has a value beyond anything else. When you think that his mind is sufficiently developed to grasp more, you can, of course, go further. You will be able to show to what lengths badness will drive bad men, that it led them to kill so good a man as Jesus for no other reason than that he refused to act in the same way as they did. Ian will, therefore, be led further to hate what is bad and to refuse to do it. In theological language he will learn to hate "sin," and all the more to love Jesus, who has given him this great example of how highly he valued a good life and how much he was prepared to suffer for the sake of good.

In this way Ian will himself become disinclined to what is wrong and inclined to good; or, again to use theological language, he will be "reconciled to God." The change from liking what is wrong to liking what is good takes place in Ian and in you and me. What we must avoid in our treatment of the meaning of the cross is the formation of any idea that the death of Jesus created any change in God and in His attitude towards men. The death of Jesus did not lead God into any position where He was more ready or more able to forgive men; since His nature or character is that of intense kindness towards us, that kindness is incapable of being changed, of being increased or lessened, or in any way affected by our behaviour or by any act of ours. The change takes place in our own attitude towards

God. Jesus is our "Saviour," though I think you will not use this term to Ian for some time yet to come, because he is the means of our "salvation," and that "salvation" comes about by our recognizing what his death was in his own conception, the asseveration in the most forcible way possible of the importance of the highest values; we, therefore, in our turn accept that standard of values, God's standard of values, as our own; our way of thinking is brought into line with God's way of thinking about life; we accept His outlook and it is we who by this change in ourselves are reconciled to Him.

If you can work out these ideas in teaching Ian about the death of Jesus, I think you will have laid a good foundation upon which he will be able to build up his own theology when he is much older, but at the same time you will not have taught him anything that afterwards he will have to unlearn. Although you will not have used any theological language, I think you will find for yourselves that this treatment of the subject is nowhere in disagreement with such phrases, upon which we were brought up, as "Salvation through the death of Christ," "Christ died for our sins," "He taketh away the sin of the world," "we are saved through faith," "Repent and be converted," and the like. It is, however, in entire disagreement, and intentionally so, with the theory of an angry and offended God needing to be appeased by the sacrifice of an innocent man who took our place as our substitute upon the cross. This theory is fatally easy and simple, but, where it is not entirely pagan, it is based upon a pre-Christian Judaism; it produces a view of the character of God so erroneous as to have possibly disastrous consequences, and it will raise subsequent difficulties in Ian's adolescent or adult mind which may lead him to reject altogether a Christianity presented to him in this shape. This "unlearning" will be almost inevitable and its danger will here be very great. The bad effect which may be created by teaching, even unconsciously, an antagonism between God and Jesus, between a Father and a son towards whom He seems to act unjustly, can be produced at a surprisingly early age. Only the other day a friend was telling me of a small boy of three or four years old whom she knew and who, because of this supposed antagonism, hated God and loved Jesus. His resentment showed itself in a curious way. He refused to say the Lord's Prayer when he went to bed, so strongly did he feel that he could not be on speaking terms with One who, as he had been taught, had forced His son to suffer. When at last under pressure he consented to repeat the prayer, he said it with the interpolation of "Fiddlesticks" at the end of each clause. The story points its own moral.

✤ VIII ✤

Hereafter

SOMETIME OR OTHER IAN WILL PROBABLY ASK YOU about death; the subject will come up in the course of conversation and he will want to know what it is. I think that whenever you speak to him about it, it may be best to link your talk to the death of Jesus, and I will therefore make a few suggestions upon it in this letter. We will be careful to say nothing that he will have to unlearn, but our difficulty is that we really know very little about death or, at least, of the state after death. That being so, it is just as well to admit our ignorance.

The subject will be made much simpler if, by the time you talk to him about death, Ian has got hold of any idea that he, his real self, and his body are two quite different, although connected, things. I think a fairly simple line of approach is to tell him that our bodies are changing every day, that they are entirely different bodies every five or seven years, although they may look the same. Yet even the appearance will change, as he will see if you show him photographs of yourselves taken a good many years ago. But all through the changes you have remained you. You may even tell him that you cut off parts of him, his nails, his hair, every week or every month; in quite a short time his nails and his hair are altogether different nails and hair. In the same way his whole body is very gradually being destroyed and built up, yet he is just the same Ian in spite of the changes. It is here that regular teaching about his physical body will come in useful, although this is not the subject I am dealing with now. For ourselves, even a small knowledge of what psychical research has very plausibly established about the possibility of the separation of the human personality from the physical body during its physical life may help us to grasp more easily the entire naturalness of the continuity of our personality after the decay of the body.

I remember that one of the books I read when I was a small boy was called *The House We Live In*; it described the wonder and the functions of the body, and I think it may help Ian if you were to describe to him his body as a house he is living in. He is not the house, he only lives in the house; the house may be altered, a new roof put on, a wing added, new paper on the walls, new furniture brought in. But none of these things are Ian; though he is in the house, yet he is quite separate from the house; one day he will probably leave the house he lives in now and live in another quite different house. But though he will then have changed his house, he will be the same Ian. Or it may even happen that for long spells of time he may be out of doors, as an explorer living in the open and sleeping under the stars, and he will then still be the same Ian. All this may serve as an illustration of the reasonableness of the idea that the body and the true self are separable, and I may remind you in passing that it is an illustration which has New Testament authority (see 2 Cor. v. 1).

Now come back to the death of Jesus. His body died and was put away in a grave; but Jesus himself remains alive; his enemies had not been able to kill him. They had only destroyed his body; they had, as it were, only pulled down his house, but they had not been able to hurt his real self (see the first part of Matt. x. 28). He remained so much alive that in some way which we cannot at all explain he made himself known to his friends, who became quite certain that he himself was not dead. All through the rest of their own lives they never had the shadow of a doubt about this. They knew that, although they could not see his face or touch his body as they had used to see and touch him, he was still really with them; although they could no longer hear words coming from his lips, yet his mind guided their minds if only they were ready to listen with their minds. Conversely they could speak and he could hear; so they quite easily formed the habit of talking with him, which they called "prayer," because he most nearly represented to them anything which they knew of God. They came to feel that in talking to Jesus they were talking to God. It was in this way, I am inclined to think, that they came to identify Jesus with God; at any rate it was only after the death of Jesus, and when they had become conscious that only his body and not he had died, that they came to recognize Jesus as God.

They came in time to see that this separation of Jesus from his body had real advantages for them. So long as he was in the body, he was tied by his body to one place at one time. If he was in Galilee and they in Jerusalem they could not communicate with him, nor he, except to an extent of which they were unconscious, with them. Now, however, it did not matter where any of them was. If Peter was in Joppa, Jesus was with him there; if John were in Jerusalem, Jesus was equally with him there; if Philip was in Samaria, he, too, knew that Jesus was with him there, just as a few years before he had actually seen him there in the same place. Once Jesus was out of the body, he was free to be anywhere and everywhere at the same time.

You will notice that I have made no reference to the "resurrection" stories. Whether they are accurate records of historical events, I am not prepared to say. With the knowledge of similar psychic possibilities which we possess, I am certainly not prepared to deny that in them and behind them lies substantial fact. The important thing is that, whether by personal experiences that happened as they are described or in some other way, the friends of Jesus were absolutely convinced that his death on the cross had not been the end of him; on the contrary they were convinced that his death, that is, the ceasing of his physical organs to function, had opened to them a new relationship with him, a new experience of him, much fuller and wider and more constant than any they had known before. Until now it had been a contact of body with body, with all the inevitable limitations of a contact of that kind. Henceforth it was a contact, a communion of soul with soul, of spirit with spirit, of mind with mind, of real self with real self, whichever word you like to use, independent altogether of any of the bonds of time or space. This is just one of many instances where, as it seems to me, the literal accuracy of the record, which was written after a considerable number of years, does not greatly matter. The essential thing is to discover the impression which was created and which caused certain experiences to be recorded, to disentangle the fact from its surroundings. This is what I have tried to convey in treating the "resurrection" of Jesus in this way.

Now, from the death of Jesus, his release, if you like to call it so, from his body, his departure from his earthly house into the full, free life of out of doors, it will be quite easy to talk to Ian about the general subject of death. Treat it as an event quite natural, as indeed it is; it is only the accompaniments of death which are sometimes horrible and which, combined with a general fear of the unknown, make us afraid of it. Death is only sad for the people who cannot immediately go with their friend. I suppose that if a whole family were to die together with all their circle of friends, and we knew all that beforehand, death would be robbed of all its sorrow and of a great part of the fear it inspires. At any rate there would be nobody left behind to wear mourning. When we make a funeral gloomy, are we not really rather selfish, pitying ourselves and thinking much more of ourselves than of the one who has gone out into a new and far greater and wider and happier experience of life? True, we need not, in a spirit of discontent, anticipate death, and in the mood of certain hymns, which I hope Ian will never sing, talk about being "weary of earth" and longing for Paradise, or singing with the angels and so forth. If life isn't good and beautiful for us, if it isn't a place where we want to stay and which we wish to enjoy, it isn't so much that life is wrong as that we are wrong in the way we handle it and look at it. But when death comes, treat it as equally good as life; if we can't do that, perhaps, then, too, there is something equally wrong in the way in which we look at it.

I have said that probably the main reason why we shrink from the fact of death and are afraid of it is that we know almost nothing about the state which lies beyond this life. This is perfectly true; and it cannot be otherwise, since so far as we can say this extension of life is on another plane; we have no words to describe

it; any ideas we may conceive of it must be hopelessly
inadequate. No one has ever come back to tell us what
it is like, and if anyone had ever returned, they would
find human speech and human minds so inevitably
limited that any true description would be quite unin-
telligible; by the nature of ourselves their story could
only very remotely approximate to reality and would
most likely create a false impression on our minds. We
must, therefore, be very careful what we tell Ian about
the after-life. You will never—it goes without saying—
talk to him about such material things as harps and
palms, golden streets and crystal seas. In any event he
has no use for them and would be very bored at a heaven
that contained them.

It does not follow, however, that you can tell him
nothing, for, so far as we can judge, there are three
principles that may guide us. The first is that we shall
continue to exist and to be ourselves, with tastes and
intelligences very much the same in kind as those we
possess here. It is, to my mind, for reasons into which
I need not enter here, very much more likely that there
is a hereafter than that there is not one, and that this
life is not all that there is of existence. It is also reasonable to suppose that on the death of the body our true
personalities will not suffer any great or sudden change,
that as our present existence has been one of continuous
and gradual development, so the same process of development will be continued, probably, we may suppose, at a
more rapid rate inasmuch as our development will not
any longer be hindered by material conditions.

Secondly, we can, I think, quite safely say, on the
assumption that God our good Father is in His nature
all that is supremely good and beautiful and true, that

the state which He wills that we shall enjoy corresponds to His nature, and that in so far as our wills have been trained to coincide with His will, in so far as we have accepted as our own these standards which we know from our acquaintance with Jesus to have been God's standards, our future existence will lie in a state of things that is supremely good. You will notice that I am emphasizing what I believe to be the natural and normal will of God for our hereafter, and I think it is along this line you could wisely teach Ian of what we call "heaven," telling him, so far as he is able to grasp the idea, that "heaven" is a spiritual state or condition of life, and is not a material place in the same sense as we talk of the seaside as a jolly place in which to spend a holiday. Heaven is not that, but, if you want a comparison, you can compare it to the "holiday feeling," the state of mind in which we feel absolutely at the top of our form. You will never be inclined, I am sure, to put into Ian's mind any pictures of the horrors of material fire and the like which used to be supposed to accompany the judgment. You will probably not say anything to him for a long time to come about any day of judgment; if we know little about heaven, we know very much less about hell; most of the popular ideas about it are derived from very crude Jewish ideas on the subject and are misleading guides for our thought to-day.

Thirdly, it will follow from the impression which you have tried to create in Ian's mind that he will learn that the death of the body—and I think the word "death" should only be used in connection with the body—is a change of life from which he need never shrink, that it is altogether a natural and normal change which sooner or later none of us can avoid. It would be foolish to be constantly talking about it, but I cannot help thinking that whenever the subject comes up in conversation, we should talk about it in an ordinary tone of voice, and not in those hushed and awed accents which in themselves are enough to excite the terrors of a childish, to say nothing of an adult, mind, for the last and worst thing you can do to a child is to create terrors for him. A child once terrified will take years before he loses his terrors, even if he can ever rid himself of them, and there is, I think, no valid reason why anyone should ever be tormented by fears.

✤ IX ✤

Miracles and Parables

I HAVE PUT ON ONE SIDE, UP TO THE PRESENT, ANY
discussion of other seemingly important incidents in
the life of Jesus and in his teaching. I have wanted that
first of all a general impression should be firmly fixed in
Ian's mind of the fact of Jesus himself and his character,
that he should first of all grasp what is easier and then
approach what is more difficult. But now we must consider a range of incidents which we may describe as
having a more unusual appearance and which cannot be
fitted so easily into our own experiences of life.

First of all the Christmas story and the birth of Jesus.
Ian already knows about Christmas. You will have already told him that on that day we keep the birthday of
Jesus, and I think that now that he has learnt of Jesus
as a grown-up man you can come back again, at some
other time than Christmas, to tell him about his birth.
In the same way as you have treated the stories of the
adult life of Jesus, you will here stick to the plain facts
of which there is no question. Jesus was once a baby,
born into a poor home, with no advantages beyond those
which other poor children have. This is at least a fact.
You may also tell how some shepherds, hearing of his
birth, came to see the baby, how later on some wise and
wealthy men came and gave him presents. How far other
and even these incidents related by St. Matthew and St.
Luke can be considered as pieces of history scientifically
understood or are not rather symbolic pictures it is im-

53

possible and unnecessary to argue. You need certainly not worry Ian's poor little brain with anything of the vexed question of the Virgin birth; for him at any rate that does not matter. He must make up his own mind upon the subject when he is much older, if it should then interest him. But for the moment stick to undeniable facts, and then add to them those stories of real beauty, whether of fact or imagination, which have been linked to them. As you will tell them to him, there is nothing in them which he will afterwards have to unlearn. The real message of Christmas is, I think, that it marks the birthday of such a wonderful person as Jesus, who has come to mean so much for us and who has changed for good the whole of human life. There, in the last analysis, I would say, lies the root of all our Christmas joy. It is because of this joy, which the world feels consciously or unconsciously, really or artificially, that we have surrounded Christmas with everything that can give happiness to other people.

Then there is a group of events which lie outside our ordinary experience of life, about which you will want to teach Ian. At least, as they are related to us in the Gospels, such happenings as the "nature miracles," the raisings from the dead, the casting out of evil spirits, are things with which we are unfamiliar to-day. At the same time that is not to say that they could not happen to-day. The more that we know of the laws of nature, the more that we are able to bring them under our control, the more impossible is it for us to say that they could not be repeated or may not be repeated in the future. If we attach any historic value at all to the records of the Gospels, it is indisputable that Jesus possessed very extraordinary powers, but at the same time there is equal evidence that in many respects his powers were not unique and were shared by others. Thus in Luke (see chapters ix. 49, x. 17, xi. 19) reference is made to the power of "casting out devils" being exercised by others, and in the Acts of the Apostles there are frequent examples of healing or even raising from an apparent state of death. It may also be said that Jesus never claimed any unique powers and never used the powers he had to attract followers to himself.

Upon the subject of the so-called "casting out of devils," you cannot, I think, do better than read the chapter in the book, *By an Unknown Disciple*, in which the story of the Gadarene swine (Mark v. 1-15) is retold and reconstructed. In this and in all the other stories of healing, we must remember that at the time at which they happened or were related there was no scientific diagnosis of disease, that there was a very deep-rooted belief in the existence and power of personal evil influences, and that anything malign and normally inexplicable was attributed to the work of these personal evil influences or spirits. Our modern diagnosis of these conditions would probably be quite different, although to a steadily increasing degree they are being referred to non-material and non-physical causes. Our present knowledge and the practice of psycho-analysis may very well be related to the "casting out of devils."

In the same way our lack of any specific or scientific knowledge of the details of the "raising" of Jairus's daughter, of the widow of Nain's son, and of Lazarus prevents us from knowing accurately what actually happened. Two things, however, I think can be said with some certainty. First, whatever happened happened in accordance with and not in contradiction of what we know as the laws of nature. We are still far from knowing all those laws, and still further from controlling them at will, but all that we know of the methods by which Jesus worked, and of those along which the will of God works, points to those methods being in line with order and not being a breach of order. The fact that these events are not within our own experience of the laws of nature does not make them impossible, but only reminds us that our observation of these laws is still incomplete. Secondly, these three instances can better be described as resuscitation, or the return of conscious life into the physical body than as any resurrection of the body. They cannot be compared with any continuance of personality after the death and decay of the body, for the bodies in these instances did not decay, and eventually all three persons had to experience that final separation of the personality from the physical body which we call death. Without further evidence, it is equally impossible to deny or to assert that they are records of suspended animation, although the effect produced both upon the recorder and the beholder was that these three persons were actually recalled from a final state of dissolution.

Last among the incidents which I have reserved and which contain certain difficulties is the group of "nature miracles," such as the feeding of the multitudes and the stilling of the storm on the lake. When I speak of difficulties in connection with these stories, you will have no difficulty in getting Ian to believe them if that is what you wish. The difficulty rather lies with yourselves, whether you can accept their literal accuracy, whether if you are doubtful about them you should teach them to Ian in a form that his later knowledge may lead him to reject, and whether you should expose him to a risk which this rejection may entail upon his whole religious experience. Like the stories of "resurrection," they run contrary to our observation of the laws of nature as we know them, and contrary to what is called by theologians or men of science "divine" or "scientific economy," which assumes, not without reason, that no extraordinary powers are called in when the same effects may be produced by ordinary means.

Once more we have to remind ourselves that the recorders of the stories wrote not only many years after the incidents they related had occurred, but also that only two of them Matthew and John, were actual witnesses of these events and that they knew nothing of trained and scientific observation. If the writer of the fourth Gospel were himself a witness of the feeding of five thousand persons, a careful reading of the whole of the sixth chapter of that Gospel may suggest that he tells the story, like other stories which he tells, not so much for its historic value as to lead his readers forward to some subsequent teaching of Jesus with which the story might be connected. To him its value appears to be more symbolic than historic. It is, therefore, suggested that all these incidents were recorded for the sake of the general impression the writer wished to convey, and I am content to believe that that is their value for us who read them to-day. For my own part I see no difficulty in believing that the hungry people were satisfied in some natural manner, either by the sharing of such food as might have been collected from the whole company or even by the disappearance of the sensation of hunger as they listened intently to the teaching of Jesus. In the same way I am content to explain the stilling of the storm and to understand that the presence of Jesus with his companions in the boat and his own complete confidence produced an equal confidence in their own minds and dispelled all their fears. I confess that I see nothing in this interpretation of these stories out of keeping with the character of Jesus, nor anything derogatory to it; on the other hand it seems, to my mind at least, to fit in more nearly with all that we know of him.

What, however, was the impression which these writers wished to make as they told these stories of the resurrection, of the feeding, of the storm? That, I think, is the question we want to ask ourselves in approaching them. We can best answer it by asking what is the impression they produce upon ourselves as we read them to-day. Is it not an impression of the extreme kindness and solicitude which Jesus showed to all who were in need of help that he could give, a kindness which was part and parcel of his whole character? It is this that stands out far more in his character than any special powers that he possessed. Other men possessed the same powers, but none the same character as he. The recorders held him up to public view not that all men should envy or attempt to imitate his powers, but that all men should seek to form their characters on his pattern, as they were inspired by his unique human expression of divine goodness.

In the same way as we seek to interpret the doings of Jesus, I think we must interpret the stories which he himself told. That is to say, I do not think we should look for any involved and elaborated meanings in them, nor for any minute explanation of the details which give colour to the stories. They were told simply to simple people; they were told in a way that would make these people think and that they would remember. A certain number of these stories speak of a judgment in some form or another; some of them are set in connection with sayings which refer to a reappearance of Jesus and a catastrophic end of the present world. All these sayings corresponded to an expectation then current among the Jews that a deliverer should arise from among them who should restore the glory and the liberty of their ancient kingdom. They expected that this deliverance would be brought to pass in a catastrophic way. It is hardly too much to say that they do not correspond to-day to any expectation of that kind. Neither you nor I believe that the way of God is catastrophic nor do we look, mainly at least, for the establishment of His kingdom in some future state of human existence. Many of the other sayings of Jesus and the general tenor of his teaching, as well as what we can observe of God's working in the world, lead us to look rather for the gradual working out of His purposes of good and the gradual transformation of mankind as the influence, the inspiration, the spirit of Jesus works upon men's personalities, and their wills are brought into unison with his. This, I think, is the general direction of his teaching, and it is in accordance with this that we have to interpret the parables and the other sayings of "judgment," quite frankly putting aside all that may have been suggested by the Jewish expectations of nineteen hundred years ago.

As we read these stories, therefore, which Jesus told, what is the general impression which they create upon us? The truth forces itself home upon us that actions and behaviour influence character, that what we do and think and say to-day has an inevitable effect upon our character, to-morrow or next year or many years hence.

What we do to-day, our outlook upon life, our attitude towards the highest values infinitely matter. We ourselves determine our own judgment, we pronounce our own sentence, we are responsible for the reckoning of the future. Clothe this idea in the language of imagery and you get the parables of the talents and the pounds, of the sheep and the goats and even that of the sower and the seed. Each is a separate illustration of the same theme. Looked at from another angle they show us the responsibility which we bear not only for ourselves but for all with whom we make contact. From the mere fact that mankind is gregarious, that each man is a unit inseparable from a larger or lesser society, it follows that for good or for evil, unconsciously or deliberately, we affect each day every other person who comes within our circle of that day. They are altered, however slightly, because we have been near them, and we are altered, too, because they have been near us. We cannot escape the responsibility of our opportunities. Is not this, in other words, the story which tells of the right and the wrong use of the talents?

I suggest that you can use the same broad method of interpretation for all the parables, looking for their message not in the specific details of each story, but in the general impression which each makes upon our mind. I am not at all sure that you may not be able to catch this general impression by reading the stories one at a time, without any preconceived idea of their meaning—although it is in the putting away of preconception that the real difficulty comes—and then as you end each story asking yourself without a moment's pause or hesitation what is the first impression that the story has made upon your mind. Remember that these stories were originally told and not read, and in the telling of a story the mind of the listener is not focussed upon the details, but upon a single point which it is the object of the teller to emphasize.

. As Ian's mind expands and is ready for more difficult teaching, I think that you will be able to tell him all these stories, using largely your own language and embroidery, especially at first, with the definite purpose of impressing upon him the one particular thing which you believe each story is meant to convey. When he gets yet older, you can talk the stories over with him again, discussing their meaning, letting him make his own suggestions and raise his own difficulties if any arise, so that they may become part of his own inheritance and make their own impression upon his life.

✠ X ✠

The Old Testament

I THINK THAT THE FIRST TIME THAT YOU AND I WERE talking of how you should teach Ian religion, we were speaking about the Old Testament; it is from that talk that anything that I have written in these letters has sprung. Up to the present I have said nothing, however, about the Old Testament, and I think you will not want me to stop without suggesting to you some ideas of how you may help Ian to understand it.

I don't know whether it has ever struck you that while you may buy a copy of the New Testament separately, you will have a good deal of difficulty in getting a separate copy of the Old. It is always bound up in one volume with the New. There is more in this fact than perhaps meets the eye at first. The New Testament is very largely a self-contained book, while the Old is not. The Old Testament is imperfect, at least for those who are not Jews, without the New; it cannot be understood without it. That is the first fact which we have to bear in mind about the Old Testament; it is an imperfect book. It is a pre-Christian book, and if we believe that the revelation of God was only given fully in the character of Jesus, of whom the records have come to us in the New Testament, it follows without any further argument that the character of God as we read it in the Old Testament is imperfectly made known to us, and that any view of God which we may gain from the Old Testament needs verifying and, where necessary, correcting by what was subsequently made known in the person and teaching of Jesus.

We must also remember that the Old Testament is a composite book or a collection of books, of varying character and covering a period of many centuries. I do not think we need discuss here the critical questions of authorship and composition; it will be enough for our present purpose if we bear in mind the general facts as I have just stated them. But the practical and natural consequence of these facts is that we must be prepared to find what indeed we do find, that there is a steadily progressive conception of God. The Old Testament begins with a very primitive conception of Him, a tribal God worshipped by a clan or a racial group, taking His place alongside the gods which were worshipped by other clans or groups. That conception rises in an ever loftier progression, and we are left with the notion of only one God to be worshipped by all men beyond that group which considered itself to be placed in a special relation to Him, who, while that group is His special possession and enjoys special privileges at His hands, nevertheless is ready to bestow privileges on certain conditions on persons outside the original group. Each generation, each century reaches to some higher appreciation of the character and personality of God through the meditation of saints and their observation of history and nature, leading them to construct a religious philosophy and way of life. But at best it was an imperfect philosophy and an inadequate way of life arising from an imperfect conception of God. Everything, therefore, that we read of the character of God, of His attitude towards man and of man's attitude towards Him must be tested by the character of God as we learn it from our knowledge of

Jesus. Where there is a conflict in the two conceptions, where there appear two standards of consequent behaviour, we must unhesitatingly discard the old in favour of the new. We cannot go back to the Old Testament as an unerring guide for our knowledge of God or for the justification of any conduct which is below the standard which is set for us in the character of Jesus.

At the same time, in any comparison of primitive religions, we find that the lowest religious ideas which appear in the pages of the Old Testament show a conception of God in the minds of the persons who are presented to us in the book of Genesis superior to that which we find elsewhere. Not the least of the signs of this superiority is to be found in its almost continuous upward progression. The Hebrew race had a genius for religious perception which other early races did not possess, and by reason of this characteristic the Old Testament occupies its high place among the early religious books of the world.

Before we go any further we should do well to remember that the books of the Old Testament were written in order to be read by the persons of the period at which they were written. They must, therefore, be interpreted in the light of whatever state of civilization or religious knowledge the writers had reached. If they were to be rewritten in the historical and religious idioms of to-day, very much that is in them would be expressed in other language. When, for example, we read the books of the prophets we have to think in the first place of the meaning which the prophets, that is the religious teachers, wished to convey to the people of their own time. That was their first purpose, and until we have been able to discover that meaning from a knowledge of the conditions of the political, social and religious life of the period, we shall fail in applying the high principles which inspired these pre-Christian writers to the entirely different circumstances of the twentieth century after Christ. If you are able to read the writings of the prophets in connection with their historical background, you will find that they gain enormously in vivid reality, and when you come to talk with Ian of these great men of the past, I should begin with this historic background, such as you can gain to some extent at any rate from a careful reading of the books of Kings. Thus you will make Isaiah a very shrewd student of foreign politics, able to forecast the probable sequence of events and to advise his king, Hezekiah, of the wise course to follow in his relations with neighbouring nations, if the king wished to preserve the security and peace of his people. In the same way you may treat the figure of Jeremiah, what at a later period definitely urged a policy of non-resistance and made himself on that account a thoroughly unpopular person in his country. Isaiah and Jeremiah will thus become living characters in history, and not mere labels attached to the top of certain pages of the Bible. You will also be able to make several of the lesser prophets, such as Amos and Zechariah, live in Ian's imagination. But at the same time you will find out from their own writings some of the social conditions of their times which in many respects are curiously like our own, and much of what they have to say about national social evils can be directly transferred, at any rate in paraphrase, to the present day.

You will, I think, be able to use the same treatment with the book of Psalms, remembering that it is an anthology, a collection of religious poetry written by many writers over a very considerable period of time. The Psalms must be understood as poetry and must be read with something of a poet's imagination. Some of them were written for the public worship of the temple and intended to be sung by choirs in responsive parts with choruses. To this group belong, for example, Pss. xcv to c, cxiii to cxv, cxviii, cxxxv and cxxxvi, cxlvi to cl. Others were written to be used on occasions of national festivals, to be recited or to be sung by a leader and chorus. This group recalls great events in the past history of the Jews, and you may take for examples, Pss. lxvi and lxviii, lxxviii, cv to cvii. A third interesting group is that of Pss. cxx to cxxxiv, known by the titles which were later appended to them as "Songs of degrees," or of steps or processions, which were sung by the pilgrims as they marched along the roads on their annual visit from the country to the temple at Jerusalem or as they climbed the temple approaches on the days of the great festival, halting perhaps on the wide platform at the head of each flight of stairs to sing a Psalm in chorus. Others, again, are entirely personal meditations or prayers which were never meant for public use and were originally perhaps never intended for the public eye; you can picture the writer using them in his own home, in moments sometimes of deep depression, at times when he knows that he has failed to express in his life the will of God as he knew it, and at other times when he could not keep silence through sheer happiness of mind. Perhaps Ian will get his first knowledge of the Psalms from hearing them sung in church, and that may serve as a good opportunity for you to talk to him about them, telling him how they were first sung two or three thousand years ago, how there has probably never been a day since when somewhere they were not being sung, telling him of all the background of each Psalm as you may know it and why they were first written, pointing out to him the beauty of their poetry, in which everything is not to be taken absolutely literally, and showing how some of their statements give a picture of the character of God which is at variance with that which we see in Christ. In passing, do not think that the titles of the Psalms have any original authority or give any clue to their authorship.

May I make suggestions now about three other books, although you will probably not introduce Ian to them until at least he has reached his teens. The book of Job is an extraordinarily interesting example of an early drama, with prologue and epilogue and six speaking characters of whom God is one. The theme is the eternal problem of the unfairness of human suffering, and various solutions of the problem are put forward. It should be read as you would read a play of the present day. "The Song of Solomon" is really a collection of several love lyrics, depicting the amours of a country girl and her lover of a higher, and perhaps royal, degree. Read in this way you will find that they have very great beauty. They are strange songs to have found their way into the Bible, but they have secured their place there because of a later fashion of mystical interpretation by which they were supposed to refer to the relations between Christ and his Church. Originally, of course, they had no meaning whatever of this kind. The book of Proverbs is a collection of common sense maxims on personal behaviour; they are full of a shrewd knowledge of human nature and, because human instincts have suffered very little integral change for more than two thousand years, they are almost all applicable as they stand to modern life. You can take Ian to them at any time, and as soon as he begins to learn anything by heart it might be quite worth while for him to store some of them in his memory. The first seven chapters are put in the form of a father's advice to his son, the eighth and ninth are a speech by a personification of wisdom, or perhaps we might say common sense of the spirit or God; the last two chapters are supposed to be spoken by a prophet and a king. These hints will give you the kind of imaginary background against which you may introduce them to Ian.

✠ XI ✠

The Old Testament Again

AFTER THESE RATHER GENERAL AND SUMMARY SUGgestions about the Old Testament, I want to discuss in more detail some of the "stories" which it contains. Some of these will present you with no difficulty; you can tell to Ian without any hesitation such tales as those of Joseph, or the call of Samuel, or the idyll of Ruth, or the early exploits of David, and some of those which are simply historical or semi-historical in the books of the Kings and the Chronicles.

Others, however, you will find real difficulty in telling him. As you face these difficulties you will bear in mind that the Bible does not set out to be a scientific treatise. Where it touches upon questions which involve matters of science for us to-day, you will remember that its writers on the one hand were attempting to put down what seemed to them or to the reciters of earlier legends, upon which they based their writings, to be a reasonable explanation of natural phenomena; that on the other, as I have already said, their knowledge of the character of God was primitive and very imperfect, although superior to that of their contemporaries or predecessors, and also that we should call them tendencious writers, that they wrote with a specific purpose to create a specific impression; therefore it should not surprise us that they did not pay great heed to our modern values of exact and scientific accuracy. Here, again, we have to read many of these stories with a poet's mind and imagination. These considerations will, I think, remove many of your preliminary difficulties, especially if you remember what I have suggested about the need of checking the religious conceptions presented in the Old Testament by their fuller development in the New and of frankly discarding as incomplete or even false—false to us, though not deliberately false in the minds of the writers—what is in conflict with this fuller knowledge which we have to-day.

Thus, for example, you will naturally never tell Ian as an historical fact, or as a fact which has any Christian value, the story of the two she-bears who ate up forty-two "little children" who had laughed at Elisha's bald head. Apart from its intrinsic improbability, this story will not do; the terrible vengeance of a prophet's curse does not fit in with the attitude of Jesus to little children or with his revelation of the good Father. We should be less shocked if the story told that the two she-bears had eaten up a prophet who lost his temper when some rude children laughed at him. The story may be classed with such bogey stories as Red Riding Hood, but even as teaching the lesson of politeness you will naturally not take it too seriously.

The story of Jonah is in a different class. Told as a "fairy story" it has a distinct fascination; told as an historic incident, it will create in Ian's mind in later years an unpleasant idea of your credulity, although I do not suppose it would upset his faith as a Christian. The story is almost certainly a parable and is intended to teach in picture form the truth, which was then only beginning to be understood and perhaps could only thus be then safely taught, that in the mind of God racial and national distinctions count for nothing; Jews and

Ninevites are alike the objects of His love. If any real incidents lie behind the story, you may perhaps understand the whale as a foreign ship, maybe a pirate ship, which picked up Jonah when he had been thrown overboard and landed him on the shore after three days. In the same way I think the stories of Daniel in the lions' den and of the three men in the furnace must be interpreted parabolically. They were written for Jews who were suffering great hardships—the lions and the furnace—at the hands of their masters in their captivity, and they were designed to encourage them to hold fast to their faith in their days of trial, and to assure them that their confidence in God's goodness would not be misplaced. The after-history of the Jews shows that these latter stories produced the effect which was intended.

Another class of difficulties will come in the earlier stories which you find in Genesis. The story of the creation, which can be paralleled by some earlier Babylonian legends, must, I think, be frankly taken as a legend, as an early and interesting attempt to produce a reasonable account of the origin of things; and to those for whom it was first written it was undoubtedly altogether reasonable. It provided them with a scheme of orderly development which had God continually behind it and which was so satisfactory to their philosophy of life that it held its place and was not generally questioned until modern times. In itself that was a great achievement, and the value of the legend even to-day is that it conceives of a world which centres around the personality of a good God. We may put it aside as not corresponding to modern scientific knowledge; but when we remember that it was never intended to be a scientific account of the origin of things, this raises no difficulty.

Yet at the same time the moral values which the first chapter of Genesis contains remain constant for us today, and that is its real wonder.

I think, too, that the difficulties which may at first appear about the "Fall" of man will disappear if you treat this story in the same way. This story is not history and as history it will not bear examination. It is again an early attempt—an attempt probably as successful as any which have been made subsequently—to explain the origin of evil. The explanation is given in the familiar primitive fashion in the form of a story, and there is no need or reason why we should take the details of the story, the garden and its trees, the serpent and the fruit, literally. This story-form was the only way in which at an early stage of human history truth could be presented and appreciated. But behind the story—and this, as I understand it, is its purpose—an eternal truth is conveyed. Man is endowed with a power of choice; it is this freedom of choice that I think makes men akin to God, or to use the language of the New Testament, "partakers of the divine nature." It differentiates man from a machine which is entirely at the mercy of a dictator-God who may be a malevolent or a benevolent despot; it raises man above the level of the other animals who are much more the captives of their instincts or circumstances. If man exercises this freedom of choice in the right direction, that is in the line of what he discovers to be the will of a good God, all is well for him; if he exercises it badly, for the satisfaction of his lower human desires, the result is misfortune and suffering whose consequences are permanent. If you thus disentangle the purpose of the story from its picturesque frame, you cannot say that this attempt to explain the problem of evil has altogether failed; at any rate it is capable of taking its place and holding its own alongside other theories which various philosophies may put forward.

I suggest, then, that in telling Ian these early stories, you should treat them frankly as legends, taking care that he shall understand that they have no scientific or historic value. But while you tell them as legends, try and get him to understand the truths which lie behind them and which it was the only purpose of the writer to convey.

The story of the flood finds its parallel in the folk lore of almost every race; some historic catastrophe, undoubtedly, lay behind these old stories. It is difficult to attach, so far as I can see, any particular moral value to it or to the story of Babel. They may stand as attempts to express early ideas of the origins of racial and tribal distribution, and if you tell them with this as their purpose, they will not only be of interest to Ian but will increase his range of knowledge.

There remains one story whose difficulty I want to deal with, the story of Abraham and Isaac. As the story is commonly told to children, I think it is apt either at the moment or later on to produce an entirely erroneous idea of God and to be a story which will have to be unlearnt. How can the God who ordered a father to kill his son be a good God? If I really accept it as a fact that God actually gave such an order as this, then the impression that I get of God is that he is bloodthirsty, that he is capable of feelings far lower than those of a human father, and that he has no relation to the good Father whom I know through Jesus. The impression which it may even convey to my mind is that I, too, may be justified in blood-thirsty acts. Of course you may put the story altogether aside as a mere legend which has no moral value. But on the other hand I am going to suggest that behind the story—whether there was a historic Abraham or not does not matter, but I do not know why there should not have been—lies a very striking landmark in the progress of the early conception of God.

If you read the whole story of Abraham carefully, you will, I think, find that the writer attaches a great importance to the place which Abraham occupies in the development of the Hebrew conception of God. Thus Abraham appears as the first of his race to break away from polytheism and as it were to discover for himself the singleness of God. This at any rate was the conviction of a later generation (see Gen. xii and Joshua xxiv. 2), and it was undoubtedly in itself a great step forward. (By the way, in reading this story we are not to suppose that such a phrase as "the Lord said" implies a visible appearance or an audible voice; it only corresponds in the vivid imagery of the language of the period to our own conviction of a strong impression that for some reason or another has come into our mind.) But this was not the only discovery that Abraham made as I suggest that we can interpret the story. Abraham was familiar in his own earlier religious practice, and in that of his acquaintances who worshipped many other gods, with the idea that the devotion of these worshippers to their gods and the means by which they could secure the gods' favour must be shown by the sacrifice of some object of value. Abraham has found his satisfaction in one God instead of many, but he will not be behind the worshippers of other gods and resolves that he will show his devotion by offering that which he prizes most. The resolve taken, there is no doubt in his mind of what the offering must be; his only son, on whom all the hopes of the family he would found were fixed, must form a human sacrifice. He goes forward to the top of a hill, the usual place of sacrifice; the preparations are being made when, like a flash, there comes into his mind the conviction that a God who would be pleased with the death of a human being was a God of a lower moral character than his own; if his own soul revolted at such an act as this, how could it be acceptable to a God to whom he must attribute moral qualities higher than those which he was conscious that he himself possessed? To use modern language we might say that here for the first time he had a vision that his God must be a God of kindness and of love, of love and kindness greater than his own. He stays his hand, but still believing in the heathen idea of a sacrifice of blood in substitution for the life of his son, a belief which persisted for centuries to come, he slays a ram upon the altar he has built. He has shown proof of his devotion and he has made the first discovery of the greatest fact in the world, that God is Love. I do not know how soon you will be able to tell this story to Ian in this way, but whenever you tell it, do not let any impression be formed in his mind that the God with whom we have anything to do could ever have sanctioned or have taken pleasure in the slaughter of human life. Tell the story, if you accept the suggestions I have made, in such a way as to show how Abraham came to believe in a good Father.

As I have gone over these stories of the Old and New Testaments, I have almost taken it for granted that you will tell them to Ian in your own words such as he can at present understand and in such a way that he will see quite easily what lies behind each story. As he grows older and as you retell the stories from time to time, I would suggest that you should gradually approximate your words to the language of the Bible itself, so that eventually he shall become familiar with the incomparable speech of the English Bible. It is true that your first aim is not to teach him that which lies at the base of modern English, but in fulfilling your greater aim, you will fulfil this other which I would almost say comes second to it.

✠ XII ✠

The Hardest Part

I HAVE ALMOST FINISHED THAT WHICH I SET OUT TO DO; I have tried as best I could to keep my promise and make some suggestions about the way in which you may teach Ian about God. But now, as I think over and read over these letters, I almost feel that I have failed in my endeavour. I have laid before you my own ideas; some of them may be of value, others may shock you by their apparent unorthodoxy. After all, however, I have left to you the hardest part, the task of passing on what I have said through the filter of your own minds. You can only teach Ian that which you yourselves believe is true, and whatever he learns he will learn best from you and Bill as his teachers.

For your own knowledge, therefore, and for your own faith, may I suggest that you should constantly try and capture the simplicity of the story that is told in the Gospels, coming to it—I confess that this is difficult—as though you had never heard it before, reading it as though it were a newly published historical novel or a newly discovered manuscript. Taken as it stands, it is really better than any of the modern so-called "lives of Christ," of which many have been written in recent years; they may have their uses, but Matthew, Mark and Luke knew their subject and their job more intimately than any modern writer. It would be good if, as we read what those early recorders wrote, we could put ourselves back, open-eyed, open-mouthed, into the first century in Palestine or Rome. At the risk, however, of being inconsistent may I make one exception and suggest that T. R. Glover's *Jesus of History* may help you to understand Jesus, for Dr. Glover has not tried to write a biography so much as to give an interpretation of a life and character in the light of the knowledge we possess to-day. In doing this, he has followed the steps of the first evangelists.

But it occurs to me that perhaps sometimes as you try to pass on to Ian what I have suggested and what you yourselves have discovered, you may be disappointed at the slowness with which your ideas seem to penetrate into his mind and express themselves in what he does. I do not think that you need be disappointed if the rate at which his religious life grows is slow. You and I probably grew very slowly mentally and spiritually, but that was so long ago that we may have almost forgotten how slow the progress was. I am sure that we ought to beware of the temptation of being impatient to see results. If you could but see the process, you would find that everything that you tell Ian each day or each week is registered in his brain, it is sinking into his mind and is gradually saturating it. What you are aiming at is to produce a character saturated and not merely tinged or colour-washed with the right idea of God, and all this is bound to take a long time. Don't force his religious growth; you are planting acorns and not mushroom spawn.

I would suggest, then, that you should not cross-examine him to-morrow about what you have tried to teach him to-day. If you are teaching him in the right way, the ideas you give him will work in him automatically. Start rather with something fresh as it were each day, almost as though you had taught him nothing before or as if you took it for granted that yesterday's talk with him had done its work, as it certainly will have done. At the same time, don't be afraid of repeating yourselves in what you say; only let the repetition, if possible, be in quite different words, with a new line of approach to the same truth which you want him to grasp. So long as you don't bore him, I think that you can't repeat the same thing too often, and you will avoid boring him if you vary your line of approach and do not too obviously try to connect it with anything you have told him before.

You will have a great many years, I hope, in which you will be teaching Ian, in which as you and he grow older you will be learning together and in which you will share with him and he with you your discoveries about God. For this reason again, I think, you will be wise not to hurry him at the start or indeed ever. Everything that you say will be locked up safely in his subconscious, if not in his conscious, mind; whatever he has learnt from you, even what you may think he has forgotten, will show itself one day when you least expect it, when perhaps you will not be at hand to see the effect of what you have taught him. In spite of all immediate appearances I am sure that what Ian is in the years to come will be very largely the result of what you are teaching him now.

I am saying all this as I bring my letters to you to an end, because I do not want you to be disappointed. I would rather that you should discount any disappointments that may for a time worry you, for you and Ian would be either more or less than human if you did not meet with moments of disappointment. Remember that nothing good that we say or do is ever wasted; it may lie dormant, but it can never die; it has an eternal life, because all good, all truth, all beauty are from God and partake of His own everlasting quality and character.

Here I end, although I know how inadequate has been my attempt to help you. If I have failed and if what I have written should prove to be of no use to you, I ask your pardon for taking up your time needlessly in reading these letters. For myself I am content that you should have given me this opportunity of teaching myself as though I were once more a child.